Dandelions

by Kathleen V. Kudlinski
photographs by Jerome Wexler

Lerner Publications Company • Minneapolis, Minnesota

To Adam Beal—growing like a weed
        —KVK

Thanks to our series consultant, Sharyn Fenwick, elementary science/math specialist. Mrs. Fenwick was the winner of the National Science Teachers Association 1991 Distinguished Teacher Award. She was also the recipient of the Presidential Award for Excellence in Math and Science Teaching, representing the state of Minnesota at the elementary level in 1992.

Additional photographs are reproduced with the permission of the following sources: © Howard Folsom/Photo Network, p. 5; © 1998 David F. Clobes/David F. Clobes Stock Photography, pp. 6, 22, 41; © Karlene V. Schwartz, pp. 7, 11(inset), 12; © Budd Titlow Naturegraphs/Visuals Unlimited, p. 8; © Cherie Winner, pp. 13, 32; © 1998 MacDonald Photography/Photo Network, p. 42. Illustrations by John Erste, pp. 23, 31, and 33.

Early Bird Nature Books were conceptualized by Ruth Berman and designed by Steve Foley. Series editor is Joelle Riley.

Website address: www.lernerbooks.com

Library of Congress Cataloging-in-Publication Data

Kudlinski, Kathleen V.
    Dandelions / by Kathleen V. Kudlinski ; photographs by Jerome
Wexler.
        p. cm. — (Early bird nature books)
    Includes index.
    Summary: Describes the physical characteristics and life cycle of
this plant, originally brought to America by English settlers to
grow in their gardens.
    ISBN 0-8225-3016-3 (alk. paper)
    1. Common dandelion—Juvenile literature. 2. Common dandelion—
Life cycles—Juvenile literature. [1. Dandelions.] I. Wexler,
Jerome, ill. II. Title. III. Series.
QK495.C74K84 1999
583'.99—dc21   98–17939

Manufactured in the United States of America
1 2 3 4 5 6 – JR – 04 03 02 01 00 99

Contents

Be a Word Detective

Can you find these words as you read about the dandelion's life? Be a detective and try to figure out what they mean. You can turn to the glossary on page 46 for help.

carbon dioxide	**minerals**	**pollen**
chlorophyll	**nectar**	**pollination**
composites	**ovule**	**rosette**
flower head	**perennials**	**taproot**

Chapter 1

A dandelion has green leaves and flowers that turn from yellow to fluffy white. How do you think the dandelion got its name?

Make a Wish

 Hold a dandelion puff close to your face. Close your eyes and make a wish. Blow at the puff as hard as you can. The tiny bits of fluff float into the wind with your wish.

Look down at the dandelion plant's leaves. They have soft, jagged edges. Long ago, people in France thought the plant's leaves looked like a lion's teeth. The French words for "teeth of a lion" are "dents de lion" (dahn-duh-lee-OHN). Say this fast, and you will see how the name became "dandelion."

The dandelion's scientific name is taraxacum officinale.

All of the plant's leaves grow from one fat, black stem. This stem is about as wide as your thumbnail. But it is shorter than an eyelash. The leaves grow in a circle around the short stem.

A dandelion's leaves grow close to the ground.

A large plant may grow 20 or more flower stems.

Taller pale green flower stems grow from the center of the plant. The stems reach up toward the sun. At the top of each stem is a tuft of golden yellow petals. That tuft holds a surprise. It isn't just one flower! Each petal belongs to a different flower. Hundreds of these tiny flowers grow at the top of one flower stem. Together, the flowers are called a flower head.

Plants with many small flowers crowded together are called composites (com-PAH-zits). Daisies, goldenrod, and marigolds are composites, too.

Goldenrod (above) *is a composite, because each of its petals is one flower. One daisy petal* (left) *is a single flower, too.*

Dandelions are not fussy about where they grow. They will grow in a large grassy field, or in a small crack in a sidewalk.

Look across a field in summer, and you'll see many dandelion flower heads. Look by roadsides and rivers. Look in yards and empty lots. It seems that dandelions are everywhere. How did they all get there?

Yellow flowers turn to white fluff in late summer.

Dandelions spread on the wind. When you wished and blew on the puff, you blew dozens of dandelion seeds into the wind. Some might land in places where they can grow. Blowing the seeds didn't make your wish happen. But it might make more dandelions happen.

Chapter 2

Fluffy dandelions blow apart and scatter their seeds. How far can the seeds travel?

The Story Begins

Each tuft of dandelion fluff has a tiny stem. A seed hangs from the end of this stem. A dandelion seed is very light. Wind can carry the fluffy tuft, its stem, and its seed for miles.

When the wind slows down, the fluff falls to earth. Tiny points on the seed stick into the dirt. The seed is ready to grow wherever there is soil and sun and water.

This tiny seed has fallen to the ground. If you look at the seed up close (inset), *you can see the points that grab the soil.*

The seed takes root and grows. Another puff of wind will blow the stem and its tuft away.

Water from rain or the soil soaks into the seed. The seed becomes soft. A small white root grows from the seed. The root is called a taproot. It turns down to the soil. It pushes into the dirt. Within a day, small hairs grow from the taproot. They are thinner than your hairs. They are called root hairs.

Under the ground, the large taproot grows straight down.

   The taproot grows down farther. Other smaller roots grow from its sides. Root hairs grow on all these roots, too.

16

Next, a short, black stem grows up from the seed. Before the stem is as long as an eyelash, bright green leaves grow from its top.

Above the ground, a stem and a few leaves sprout.

At first there are just two leaves. Then more leaves grow. Soon leaves crowd the top of the stem. As the leaves keep growing, they spread out in a circle. Now the plant looks like a jagged green rose. This is called a rosette (roe-ZET).

This potted dandelion spreads its leaves in a perfect rosette.

The leaves grow close together, so no other plants can grow near the dandelion.

The rosette's leaves make a circle of shade beneath them. If other seeds blow into the shade circle, they cannot grow. The dandelion does not have to share its soil and water with other plants, so it grows fast. The dandelion pushes its taproot deeper into the dirt. And the plant grows more bright green leaves.

Chapter 3

Leaves from two different dandelion plants might have different shapes. But they are both green. Do you know what makes leaves green?

A Special Green

Green plants like dandelions have chlorophyll (KLOR-uh-fihl) in their leaves and stems. Chlorophyll makes plants green. But chlorophyll does much more than make color. Chlorophyll makes food for growing plants.

Your skin may be brown or black, tan or pink. But it is not green. You have no chlorophyll. You have to eat food to stay alive. Most plants do not have to eat. Their chlorophyll makes food from sunshine, water, air, and minerals (MIN-ur-uhls). Minerals are things that come from the soil.

Sunshine helps chlorophyll make food for all green plants.

If you cut a dandelion stem, you will see that it is hollow.
Water travels through the stem walls.

Minerals go into a plant's roots with water. There are tiny tubes inside a dandelion's roots. The tubes run from the tips of the root hairs and through the plant's stems. They go to every leaf in the dandelion plant. The plant sucks water and minerals through these tubes.

Air is all around a dandelion plant. Part of the air is carbon dioxide (dy-AHK-side). Air goes into the dandelion's leaves through tiny holes. Inside the leaves, carbon dioxide joins the water and minerals that come up through the roots. Chlorophyll turns the carbon dioxide, water, and minerals into food. Chlorophyll needs energy to make food for the plant. That energy comes from sunshine.

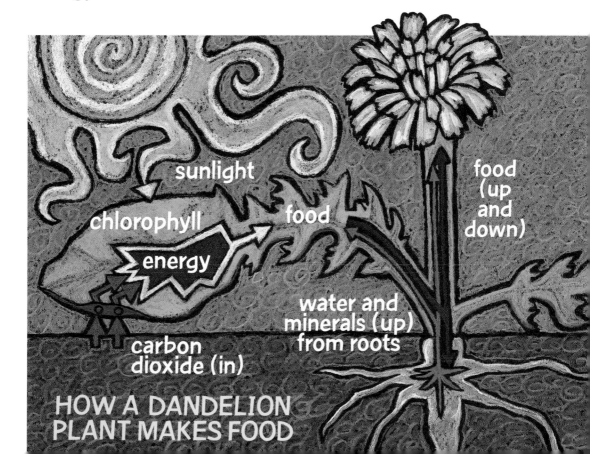

sunlight

chlorophyll   food

energy

food (up and down)

water and minerals (up) from roots

carbon dioxide (in)

HOW A DANDELION PLANT MAKES FOOD

A dandelion's roots store extra food to protect the plant.

A dandelion plant uses most of the food it makes to grow strong and tall. It sends some of the food back into its roots. The extra food stays in the dandelion's taproot.

A hungry rabbit may eat a dandelion's leaves. Or a lawnmower may cut the rosette off. But the plant will not die. The root can use its stored food to start a whole new dandelion plant.

In our yards, dandelions are weeds. They are hard to get rid of, because the roots are strong.

Chapter 4

A dandelion bud holds many tiny flowers inside its leaves. Do you know how many flowers are inside the bud of one flower head?

The Lion's Mane

 Dandelions make their flower heads early in the spring. Each flower head begins as a bud. The bud is covered with two layers of special leaves. The bud's stem grows and lifts the bud up toward the sun.

One sunshiny morning, the bud opens. Dozens and dozens of tiny yellow flowers bloom. One flower head may have 200 flowers. By late afternoon, the flower head closes again. It opens and closes for three or four days. Then it closes for good.

The dandelion bud waits for the sun to shine, then it opens. It closes when the sun goes down.

Here a petal has unrolled (right). *It has separated from the stalk* (left). *The stalk is covered with pollen.*

While the flower head is open, each flower's petal unrolls. A tiny stalk pokes out. This stalk is covered with yellow dust called pollen. Each speck of this dust is one grain of pollen. One pollen grain is needed to make each seed.

Deep inside each flower is a tiny drop of sweet tasting juice. This juice is called nectar. Below the nectar is an ovule (AHV-yool). The ovule will grow into a seed if a grain of pollen reaches it.

This dandelion flower head has been cut away. Can you see the ovules, which will become seeds?

There are two ways that pollen can reach an ovule. Sometimes an insect can help. An insect may visit a flower to drink the sweet nectar inside. The insect pushes its head into the dandelion's flower head to drink. The insect gets pollen on its feet and face.

Bees, butterflies, wasps, and other flying insects drink the nectar inside a dandelion's flowers.

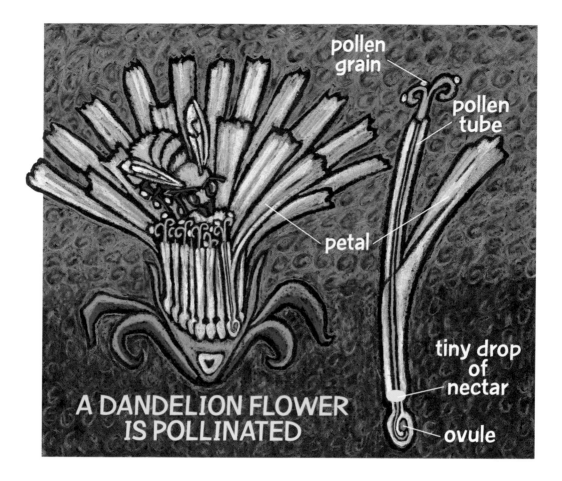

pollen
grain

pollen
tube

petal

tiny drop
of
nectar

ovule

A DANDELION FLOWER
IS POLLINATED

The insect walks across the flower head. Some of the pollen stuck to the insect's body brushes off. If a pollen grain is moved to the tiny tip of a flower's stalk, a thin tube starts to grow from the grain. When a tube grows down to reach an ovule, this is called pollination (pohl-ih-NAY-shun). A pollinated ovule grows into a seed.

As long as this bud stays closed, insects cannot pollinate the plant. Its flowers will pollinate themselves.

Sometimes an insect can't pollinate a dandelion. If the sun doesn't shine for days, the flower bud stays closed. No insects can get inside to move the pollen. This doesn't bother the dandelion. Inside the closed bud, pollen grains grow tubes. The tubes find the ovules. The dandelion flowers pollinate themselves in the darkness of the closed bud.

A pollinated flower bud stays closed. Tiny seeds form inside the bud. The seeds are safe in a part of the bud that is shaped like a cup. The seeds grow bigger.

DANDELION SEEDS GROW

seeds

Each seed sprouts a tiny stalk and a tuft of fluff. Later that fluff will help the seed fly. The seed stores food to use when it first starts to grow. A hard coat grows around the seed. The coat will keep the seed safe on its trip through the air. Sharp points grow on the seed coat.

These seeds have grown to full size. Each seed is covered with a hard brown coat.

The seeds and their tufts are pushed out to form a perfect, fluffy ball.

Now the bud's stem begins to grow. It pushes the bud up high, into the wind. On a dry day, the bud opens for the last time. The cup holding the seeds turns inside out.

A breeze can now catch the silky tufts and blow the seeds into the air.

The flower head has turned into a fluffy seed head. Maybe it is the one you made a wish on and blew apart!

Chapter 5

All of these plants did not grow in just one summer. What is a plant called that grows year after year?

A Rose in Winter

Many plants live only one summer. A dandelion can live for many years. Plants that live year after year are called perennials (puh-REN-ee-uhls). Each summer, the dandelion plant makes hundreds of seeds to send out on the wind.

A dandelion's leaves die in the fall, just like the leaves on a tree.

When summer is over, the days grow short and cold. Dry winter winds begin to blow. The dry wind chaps your lips and sucks the water out of leaves. Cold winds freeze the water left in leaves. Without water, chlorophyll can't make food to keep a green plant alive.

Most dandelion leaves die, but not the whole plant. The dandelion grows a new rosette. This winter dandelion is small and flat. It stays out of the dry, cold winds. It does not need much water or sun to stay alive. When spring comes, the dandelion has a head start. It is ready to grow, long before other plants. The dandelion goes right to work, making more dandelions.

Through the coldest winters, dandelions stay alive and wait for spring.

Chapter 6

Dandelions did not always grow in North America. Where did dandelions come from?

Why Is It a Weed?

Hundreds of years ago, there were no dandelions in North America. Then people began moving to North America from England. The English people brought dandelions with them to plant at their new homes. They planted dandelions in gardens, to grow for food.

They ate young dandelion leaves in salads. They boiled larger leaves before they ate them. They dried dandelion roots and ground them up. They used the ground-up roots to make a drink like coffee. They even used dandelion flower heads to make a sweet wine.

Some people still eat dandelions. If you eat dandelion greens, do not pick them from an area that has been fertilized or sprayed with poisons.

A single dandelion plant won't be alone for long. In just a few years, one plant can become a field full of dandelions.

Those English farmers didn't waste the dandelion seeds on wishes. They saved them to plant again. But some of the seeds flew out of their gardens. Soon wild dandelions grew everywhere, spreading more and more of their seeds on the wind.

Most people don't plant dandelions anymore. The wind does that for us. Dandelions grow in our lawns and gardens. Dandelion rosettes make shadows where grass and other plants can't grow. When dandelions are in our way, we call them weeds. But dandelions haven't changed. They're still trying to make as many more dandelions as they can.

We can try to keep these weeds out of our yards. But dandelions are here to stay.

On Sharing a Book

As you know, adults greatly influence a child's attitude toward reading. When a child sees you read, or when you share a book with a child, you're sending a message that reading is important. Show the child that reading a book together is important to you. Find a comfortable, quiet place. Turn off the television and limit other distractions, such as telephone calls.

Be prepared to start slowly. Take turns reading parts of this book. Stop and talk about what you're reading. Talk about the photographs. You may find that much of the shared time is spent discussing just a few pages. This discussion time is valuable for both of you, so don't move through the book too quickly. If the child begins to lose interest, stop reading. Continue sharing the book at another time. When you do pick up the book again, be sure to revisit the parts you have already read. Most importantly, enjoy the book!

Be a Vocabulary Detective

You will find a word list on page 5. Words selected for this list are important to the understanding of the topic of this book. Encourage the child to be a word detective and search for the words as you read the book together. Talk about what the words mean and how they are used in the sentence. Do any of these words have more than one meaning? You will find these words defined in a glossary on page 46.

What about Questions?

Use questions to make sure the child understands the information in this book. Here are some suggestions:

> What did this paragraph tell us? What does this picture show? What do you think we'll learn about next? Where do dandelions grow? How are dandelions similar to other plants? How are they different? How far can a dandelion seed travel? How does a dandelion make its own food? How do insects help dandelions? How did dandelions get their name? What is your favorite part of this book? Why?

If the child has questions, don't hesitate to respond with questions of your own, such as: What do *you* think? Why? What is it that you don't know? If the child can't remember certain facts, turn to the index.

Introducing the Index

The index is an important learning tool. It helps readers get information quickly without searching throughout the whole book. Turn to the index on page 47. Choose an entry, such as *wind,* and ask the child to use the index to find out how wind helps dandelions grow. Repeat this exercise with as many entries as you like. Ask the child to point out the differences between an index and a glossary. (The glossary tells readers what words mean, while the index helps readers find information quickly.)

All the World in Metric

Although our monetary system is in metric units (based on multiples of 10), the United States is one of the few countries in the world that does not use the metric system of measurement. Here are some conversion activities you and the child can do using a calculator:

WHEN YOU KNOW:	MULTIPLY BY:	TO FIND:
miles	1.609	kilometers
feet	0.3048	meters
inches	2.54	centimeters
pounds	0.454	kilograms
gallons	3.787	liters

Activities

Dandelion leaves and flowers make bright colors when rubbed on paper. Color a picture of a dandelion using its own parts.

Think about a device you could make to carry you in the wind. What would it look like? How would you attach it to your body? What would you use to build it? Draw a picture of your invention and describe how it works.

Play a game with dandelion seeds. Blow on a seed that is attached to a white tuft. Notice how the seed moves. Does it stay at the same height as it moves? What makes it rise higher or sink down? Can a seed that has fallen to the ground rise back up without being touched? Have a "seed race" with others. To start, all the racers must blow on their seeds at the same time. Do all the seeds end up in the same place?

Glossary

carbon dioxide (dy-AHK-side)—a part of air that plants use to make food

chlorophyll (KLOR-uh-fihl)—the green substance found in a plant that makes food for the plant

composites (com-PAH-zits)—plants with many small flowers clustered together in heads

flower head—a cluster of tiny flowers

minerals (MIN-ur-uhls)—things found in the soil that are not plants or animals

nectar—a sweet liquid that flowers make

ovule (AHV-yool)—a baby seed

perennials (puh-REN-ee-uhls)—plants that live for more than one year

pollen—a flower's yellow powdery grains

pollination (pohl-ih-NAY-shun)—the joining of ovules and pollen to make seeds

rosette (roe-ZET)—a cluster of leaves that looks like a flat rose

taproot—a thick root that grows straight down

Index

Pages listed in **bold** type refer to photographs.

The Early Bird Nature Books Series